More Than Enough

The Healing Journey to
Love Yourself,
Listen to Your Gut &
Live Your Truth

By Dr. Riva Z. Robinson

This book is for Grandma and Granny: two of the most inspiring women who ever lived. You both left an incredible legacy, and I can feel you smiling down on me as I now create my own.

Table of Contents

Introduction

A storm of anxiety immediately flooded my mind the moment I seriously committed to writing this book.

What on earth am I going to wear for the cover photo of my book? I need to look really polished... maybe I'll wear my pearls! But will that look too pretentious?

Which photographer am I going to work with? I need someone who's rrrreally good, and can make me look rrrreally good... but how much is that going to cost? It doesn't matter; I need to have the best!

And who's going to do my makeup? I can't possibly do it myself - people looking at the cover will know!

Oh man, I'm actually going to have to wash my hair... Okay, so I'll schedule my photoshoot for a weekend day when I have more time to tame this mess on my head.

With just three weeks before my book launch, and still nothing settled for my book cover, I found myself at a networking event. It had completely escaped my mind that a photographer would be there taking free headshots.

SCORE... I could use these shots for my book! But wait, I'm not wearing any makeup! CRAP!

I quickly realized that this couldn't be more perfect! My book is called "MORE than Enough," and what better opportunity than this to practice living my truth, here and now.

So I posed in my go-to double bicep pose, big cheesy smile, no makeup, hair unwashed for a week, wearing my $10 six-year-old little black dress, feeling 100% me.

I can't be the person just talking the talk; I need to walk the walk and live my truth. It's as vital to my survival as the oxygen I breathe. When I show up as myself in raw form, I'm 100% alive.

I don't need makeup to be beautiful when I've been blessed with flawless skin and a radiant smile. I don't need fancy clothes and jewelry, when I love my body and believe it is perfect on its own. And I don't even need a professional photographer, when I've got portrait mode on my iPhone X.

I am enough.

CORRECTION

I am MORE than enough!

You may be reading this thinking, "Wow, Dr. Riva is so confident!" But, let me tell you... that was not always the case. This has been a journey.

There was a time when I absolutely HATED my body. Loathed it. Felt tormented living in it. I thought my legs were so appallingly fat that I even fantasized about having them amputated.

And now, I can glide across the stage of my latest national bikini competition in a tiny Swarovski crystal bikini, owning every inch of my body, and especially loving my well-developed muscular legs.

Anything is possible. If I can overcome my insecurities, so can you.

But this isn't a book just about loving your body; it's about loving yourself fully and completely.

It is about the healing journey to love yourself, listen to your gut, and live your truth, so that you can embody one of the greatest truths of all: that you are More Than Enough.

A funny thing happened when I started writing this book. I was positive that it would be a book about physical health. This definitely plays a role in the book, yes, but what will unfold in the coming pages is not what you would expect from a traditionally-trained Western Medicine physician.

As the words started to flow through me and onto the pages, I saw clearly what this book, my mission, and my life are all about.

Self-Love.

If you could hear the recording that played in my head for most of my life, it would sound something like this:

I'm not skinny enough.
I'm not good enough.
I'm not pretty enough.
I'm not popular enough.
I'm not smart enough.
I'm not rich enough.
I'm not White enough.
I'm not Black enough.

Rewind. Press Play. Repeat again... NEVER enough.

Not-Enoughness is something I've struggled with for as far back as I can remember. Just when I think I have it fully conquered, it attacks me in a different way.

I know it's never going to disappear completely, and that is why I have developed the mindset, tools, and strategies to prevent this Not-Enoughness from taking over my life.

Because I now know at my core that I am More Than Enough, PERIOD. That old dialogue does not hold me prisoner anymore.

But in order for us to defeat Not-Enoughness, we have to know exactly what it is we're fighting.

To help us get to know Not-Enoughness, I have identified five ways that it manifests in our lives.

The 5 Manifestations of Not-Enoughness are:

1. **Poor Body Image**
2. **Perfectionism**
3. **Settling For Less**
4. **Seeking External Validation**
5. **Denying Your Dreams**

You might have noticed that there is some overlap between these five items. Just as our human body is a complex system of interdependent organs, so are the inner workings of our minds.

Is this hitting home yet?

I know I feel a little squirmy in my chair, and I hope you feel a little bit uncomfortable, too. I hope you get so uncomfortable reading this book and hearing all of the stories, that you finally are fed up with living a life of LESS THAN, and start to fully embrace a life of MORE THAN ENOUGH.

This is your one and only precious life that you have to live. It's time to start the healing journey to love yourself, listen to your gut, and live your truth.

You deserve it. You are worth it.

You are good enough.
You are strong enough.
You are wise enough.
You are MORE than enough.

Yours always in Enoughness,

Dr. Riva

Section 1:

Five Manifestations of Not-Enoughness

Chapter 1: Poor Body Image

As a young gymnast, I was a solid hunk of muscle. My nickname was even "Riva the Rock." What six-year-old has rock-hard six pack abs and massive biceps that could make a grown man think twice about crossing her? *This girl.*

But when I looked in the mirror, what did I see? ALL fat. I even remember the exact moment it dawned on me that I labeled myself as "fat." I was four. Standing in line to do my tumbling pass across the floor, I scanned my teammates' bodies up ahead. None of their thighs touched.

My thighs weren't just kissing; they were married for life!

And none of them had a bubble butt like I did. *My coach would scream across the gym, "Riva, tuck your butt under!"* And any of you who have done dance or gymnastics and have a big booty know just how impossible a demand like that is! My big black behind wasn't going under.... around the side... east... or west. It was staying perched high at full salute - no matter what.

I became a victim of my "fat." Anytime I couldn't perform a move properly, it was because I was "too fat." I pinched and pulled and slapped at my imaginary rolls of fat, praying desperately for God to melt them away.

Of course, when puberty hit, things didn't get any better. The stretch marks and cellulite that suddenly appeared weren't just physical blemishes; I felt as if my soul was forever tarnished. I couldn't believe how far I'd "let myself go." To say I hated my body was an understatement. I felt cursed.

And so began the constant cycle of dieting... Atkins... South Beach... The Master Cleanse. *Those are healthy, right? Carbs are evil and those who consume them shall be forever banished to an eternity of fatness...* or so I thought.

By the time I got to college, the pursuit of skinniness ruled my every thought. Mind you, this was also when America's Next Top Model was at its peak. So, between practicing my "smize" and my model walk, I'd peruse pro-anorexia websites for their "expert tips."

Up 5 pounds, down 10. Up 12 pounds, down 8. Starve. Binge. Repeat.

Then, I had a breakthrough.

I took a nutrition course during my sophomore year, and my whole world turned upside down in the best of ways. My professor was an intelligent, strong, confident, compassionate, super-fit woman who had mastered food! Her passion was palpable and her knowledge irrefutable - food wasn't the enemy after all!

As obsessed as I had been with banishing foods to starve myself thin, I became even more obsessed with harnessing food's power to restore balance within. I started to no longer use food to fill an emotional hole; it actually made me feel whole! This was a freedom that I had never imagined to be possible.

Now, I'd be lying if I said that my poor body image just *POOF* disappeared. Oh, HELL no! I know that it will be a lifelong struggle to not have my self worth attached to my body, but I also know that beyond a shadow of a doubt, this struggle will never completely consume me again.

I know my triggers, and I avoid them. I know what makes me feel good about myself, and I seek more of that. And I am beyond blessed to have a husband who constantly affirms me (and what I already know to be true about myself!) *How did I get so lucky?!*

You may be surprised by this, but venturing into the world of bodybuilding and bikini competitions has actually helped me heal and love my body even more. And it is not because I'm now in the best shape of my life... it is so much more than that! It is because I now have a whole new respect and appreciation for what a marvelous creation the human body is!

In August 2018, I had my heart set on competing in the Fit Expo Anaheim bikini competition, right next door to Disneyland. *Need I say more?*

Ideally, my competition preparation consists of at least 12 weeks of training, and preferably 16 weeks, but this time around, I only had nine weeks! Not only that, but I had just come off of a three-week vacation in Thailand, where I literally ate everything within my hand's reach. Come Day 1 of prep for the competition, I was starting out eight pounds heavier than my normal weight, but with almost half as much time to reach my peak physique.

It seemed impossible, but I was determined. I pushed myself harder than ever before, but also showed myself more compassion than ever before, too. I tapped into the power of my mind and constantly visualized the beautiful transformation my body was undergoing. I literally would talk to my muscles as I worked out and thanked them for getting stronger and leaner.

Any time I wanted to give up (especially when it came time for my cardio sessions), I would repeat over and over, "I'm so happy and grateful that I'm the Overall Bikini Champion of Fit Expo Anaheim." I would hear the judges call out my name, feel the crown on my head, and the joyful, triumphant feelings would wash over me. Instantly, my energy would change. *All right Stairmaster, let's do this!*

I was so obsessed and possessed by my vision that my body had no choice but to submit to it. It was astounding, but not the least bit surprising, to see the rapid, remarkable transformation of my physique!

For years, my mind had kept my body trapped because all I fed it was thoughts of how fat and ugly I was. All of a sudden, I was using my mind to liberate my body to express itself in the fittest form possible.

Any guesses for who won that show?

More Than Enough Message #1

On Defeating the Not-Enoughness of Poor Body Image

You were created perfect. Whether you believe in God or another higher power or nothing at all, there are no accidents. You are who you are for a reason. Blemishes and all.

Just think how remarkable your body is for a minute. You are breathing right now and you don't have to think about how the oxygen is being extracted from the air in your lungs, and eventually into your blood, and then into every cell of your body to keep you alive. You are a marvelous, miraculous creation, no matter what form your external body takes.

No one gets it more than I do, that you might want to modify your body. That's fine. You deserve the chance to be the best version of yourself, inside and out. But remember, your body is just a vessel. It only manifests whatever energy you put into it - and it's not just food I'm talking about. It's your thoughts, too.

If you want a body that you love, you must first feed it loving thoughts.

Chapter 2: Perfectionism

Do I really want to be a doctor?

I tried my best to uproot that tormenting thought, but like a pesky weed it kept springing up again, each time burrowing deeper into my mind.

This has always been the plan. Don't think too much and ruin it all now!

On a silver platter was the perfect opportunity to have the perfect life that would be the greatest pride of my parents and the most bitter envy of my perfect friends.

I could be accepted to medical school... in high school!

Yep, I was one of those freakishly smart kids in high school who didn't just get a perfect score on the exam. I completed all of the bonus assignments to get extra credit so I could be MORE than perfect.

Like an architect, I crafted an impeccable blueprint for my flawless future. A 4.3 GPA with obscenely high scores in Math and Science - *Check.* Star performer on the gymnastic team - *Check.* Leader in all of the eye-catching extracurriculars and community service activities - *Check. Check, Check, Check.* I couldn't have looked more perfect on paper.

So, naturally, when I discovered that the prestigious Rice University in Houston had a dual acceptance program with Baylor College of Medicine, that was my next conquest. But for some horrible reason, I couldn't shake the lingering doubt and the constant worrying about whether this was the right choice for me or not.

Why was I feeling this way?!

Medicine was practically encoded in my DNA as the child of two physician parents. At the age of three, I was essentially inducted into the profession when they gave me a Fisher-Price doctor's kit for Christmas. *Remember that one?* It was a little black doctor's tote, complete with all of the miniature essentials - a stethoscope, a reflex hammer, a shot, a cast, and bandages. As a child, I saw my parents as Supreme Beings, and now with this little kit, I had joined their ranks.

Over the years, the cracks on the "perfect" surface of a doctor's life exposed what felt like a less-than-perfect core. I'd witnessed the long hours my parents had worked and the struggles of owning and operating their own medical practice. Countless times, I was the last one at school or gymnastics, waiting for my parents to pick me up, or the only one whose parents weren't present for a special event. It was sad and embarrassing, of course, but I understood my parents' hard work was the necessary sacrifice that enabled us to live richly.

With all of this informing my decision-making process, I was hit with a sudden thought that knocked the wind out of me before I even knew what happened.

Maybe I could do things differently than them?

That thought was like a sucker punch. My whole existence had centered around conforming exactly to what my parents, teachers, coaches, or judges had expected of me. I knew exactly what to do to be perfect. There was a very simple formula to it: just do what they tell you to do!

I had no idea how to operate beyond this paradigm. It felt debilitating.

So I did what so many of us do in a bind: I made a bargain with God.

Okay God, if I get into the Rice-Baylor Medical Scholars Program, then I'll become a doctor. If I don't get in, then I'll figure something else out.

You can probably guess how that turned out. That's right, I got in. *Check.* Of course, I was elated to have been accepted - it was a major accomplishment! Another high honor and badge of success to add to the wall of trophies, plaques, medals, and ribbons that validated just how perfect I was. But a not-so-small part of me was mortified.

*Am I really doing this? *Gulp**

My years at Rice dealt a series of sucker punches that left me floored time and time again.

Until then, my entire identity and self worth had been wrapped up in being the perfect student. When I realized at midterms I was failing Organic Chemistry, my whole world and sense of self crumbled. *What has happened to me?! OMG, I'm going to get kicked out of Rice-Baylor... I might as well drop out of school... my parents are going to disown me... my life is over...*

Fortunately, I ended up with a C by the end of the semester, and I wasn't dismissed from the program or disowned by my parents. But, the perfect A+

transcript I'd been building up since first grade was forever tarnished.

Having the perfect academic career certainly wasn't possible anymore... and it was a good reminder that life was not just about having perfect grades.

What perfect timing for this realization! I had just signed up for a cool, new website called "The Facebook!" Now I could divert my attention to posting an endless photo reel of just how perfect my life was. *LIKE*

Watch out! Here comes another sucker punch of Not-Enoughness...

Everyone else has a more perfect life than I do! Like, that girl from my Psych class... she's dating that hot baseball player, she's always wearing designer EVERYTHING, and she's so skinny. I hate her!

I'd never had a boyfriend and was convinced I was doomed to roam the earth alone. I had no money for designer *anything*. Everytime I wore my knock off Seven jeans, I was so paranoid I'd be called out as an imposter. And if you peeked into my mind and read my self-hating internal dialogue, you would have thought I were morbidly obese.

If I was conscious and breathing, I was comparing myself to someone. It was an exhausting but sickeningly intoxicating obsession. Any time I saw someone with their legs exposed, my eyes would immediately scan their knees and register how much knee fat they had, and the thoughts would stream in.

Final tally: nobody has as much knee fat as I do. If only I was skinny and had knobby knees, maybe I'd have a hot baseball player boyfriend, too. And he'd love me enough to buy me a real pair of Seven jeans. And then my life would finally be perfect.

My idea of a "perfect" life was a hot boyfriend, nice things, and skinny legs.

Skip ahead a couple of years, and fate had turned in my favor towards this "perfect" life - I finally had a boyfriend! A hot *European* one, at that! *And "nice things" would be sure to follow, right?*

The next chapter, "Settling for Less," divulges the juicy tale of my dysfunctional relationship with Jacques, but you can infer from the title how it worked out. I'll just say that my calculations were not correct.

It turned out that my hot European boyfriend wanted nice things, too, which were often on my dime.

Jacques was handsome and charming and exotic on the surface, but he had an antagonistic and spiteful nature that would erupt without a moment's notice. I shrank and submitted and would do anything to appease him. It was the price I was willing to pay to avoid being alone.

But, have no fear, Facebook is still here! I flooded my feed with all of the perfect pictures of our worldwide adventures, proving just how perfect our life together was! Although I was losing myself in that all-consuming relationship, I found so much gratification from my friends' jealous comments. "How do you take a week off in the middle of the term to travel around Europe, Riva?! You have the best life!"

Shhh, don't tell anyone, but my "best life" is actually a heaping pile of shame, fear, and insecurities perfectly masked by our perfect, sun-tanned, smiling faces on postcard-worthy beaches.

Eventually, my relationship with Jacques imploded (don't worry, the full soap opera continues in the next chapter), and I was left to channel perfectionism in another way...

Are you noticing a trend in the Not-Enoughness?

The writing of this book led me to one massive realization: relentlessly chasing perfection had always been the focal point of my existence.

Whether it was my body, my academic career, my social life, or my relationships, I invested every fiber of my being into the pursuit of perfection. My identity became consumed by an unrealistic ideal, and when I failed to reach it, I was left not knowing who I was or what I truly wanted. To put it simply, I was lost. *Lost in the pursuit of perfection.*

The thing about the pattern of perfectionism is that once you are in it, if the pattern goes unaddressed, it just keeps manifesting.

So, even after going to medical school, the opening dilemma of this chapter came back around.

Did I really want to be a doctor?

By this point in time, I'd survived the worst parts of school, so there was no doubt I'd be graduating with my medical degree. But, there was no specialty that I truly loved, and I knew from my own childhood experience that I wanted a different lifestyle than my parents.

Maybe I'll do Dermatology. It's boring as hell, but they make a lot of money without having to work long hours. So I can have the quality of life that I want outside of my work. Nobody really loves their work anyways. The perfect life doesn't come without compromising something...

Well, I didn't have to compromise and go into Dermatology because I wasn't accepted into a residency program for it. Fortunately, I did get matched up with my first choice for my intern year in New York, and I couldn't have been more excited about that!

As luck would have it, my hospital was in one of the roughest neighborhoods in the South Bronx, and I hated every minute I was within those walls. Determined as I was to create the perfect work-life balance, I counteracted my workday misery with nightlife debauchery. *Mom, you always taught us to work hard, play hard!*

I have no earthly idea how I survived that year. I'd still be burning up the dancefloor at 3 o'clock in the morning when I had to be rounding on patients at 6 o'clock. My blood probably had greater parts Red Bull and alcohol than blood itself. I tried to convince myself that this was the life I wanted, but it felt so empty... *I felt so empty*. My voice reverberated through my shell of a body in an infinite echo, as I pondered, *what has happened to me?* I was nowhere to be found.

No words can begin to do justice to the significance of what happened next.

Life-changing... earth-shattering... soul-stirring... mind-blowing... awe-inspiring... they all seem too trite. None big enough or deep enough or wide enough to accurately describe the greatest sucker punch of my life - one I would welcome again and again again.

I was home in Texas visiting my family for Christmas, and my friend James invited me to a rave with a group of his friends. There was one guy in particular who stood apart from the rest - Sean. Like me, he was home visiting his family for the holidays. Once we hit the dancefloor together, the rest was history.

We literally fell in love as we danced the night away, and we've been inseparable since then, even though we spent the first one and a half years together in a long-distance relationship.

When I met Sean, it was as if my heart exploded as it swelled with a love so intense it ripped right through me. All of my self-protective defenses: shattered. All of my facades of perfection: faded. He saw straight to the core of me - battered, bruised, and wounded - and he embraced me. He even loved me. *How is it possible for him to love me as I am, and I can't love myself this way?*

I caught a glimpse of my reflection in Sean's adoring eyes and saw a blurry silhouette of a woman worth loving. *Is that really me?* I had long avoided any kind of deep self-exploration, fearing what hidden, ugly truths I'd discover underneath my surface.

Without a shadow of a doubt, I knew Sean was my other half. But, I was so badly fractured and scarred that I wasn't even a whole half. It was obvious I needed to do the healing work on myself before our two halves could be united seamlessly. It was my responsibility alone to shake my Not-Enoughness and grow into the worthy woman we both deserved to love.

I'll tell you, growth isn't easy or quick... and often, it's not pretty or fun, either. But my dear reader, it is worth it. It is so incredibly worth it.

All my life I yearned for a man's love that would "fix" me and all of my problems, when it was truly my own love I sought. Everything I'd ever wanted was already within me. I was always worthy; I simply needed to accept it.

Talk about a mind-blowing revelation! If I was worthy of love, perhaps I was worthy of fulfillment in my career, too? Sean and I were on track to create a beautiful life together, and I didn't want any of my career dissatisfaction corrupting the sacred, blissful space of our relationship.

Even still, I was confused as to what an alternative path in Medicine might look like. All I knew was that I wanted to focus on wellness and helping people thrive instead of just helping people "get by."

I yielded to my parents' strong suggestion to continue with a specialty residency, buying into the rationale that being board-certified would grant me more authority as a physician. As convinced as I was of my self-worth, I was still too afraid to stray from the tried-and-true traditional route in Medicine. *I didn't come this far to not be a well-respected doctor!*

So, I made what I thought was a worthy compromise. I settled on following up my intern year with the shortest possible residency program I could find that seemed related to wellness - Preventive Medicine. *If I "have to" do this, then at least it's only two years... I can survive another two years.*

What had started out as a smoldering gut feeling - *maybe this isn't right* - grew into a five alarm fire - *RUN FOR YOUR LIFE, RIVA!*

Uncontrollable crying spells seemed to erupt from the depths of my soul. Skull-splitting migraines "mysteriously" raged in intensity the closer I got to campus. Unrelenting nausea and gastrointestinal upset constantly sent me scrambling to the nearest bathroom. Inexplicable searing hot pains migrated across my body.

Every fiber of my body was in revolt of my decision to conform to what I thought was "right."

But what's "right" isn't always right for you.

If I'd seen a regular doctor, I probably would have been diagnosed with depression, irritable bowel syndrome, and fibromyalgia. But "oddly" enough, all these symptoms suddenly went away when I was with Sean.

After only three months in the Preventive Medicine residency, I resigned.

I kid you not, it was the most terrifying thing I've ever done.

But also, the most gratifying. I was finally free. *Scared stinkless... but free!*

Without the deafening "have to's" and the "should's" ringing in my ears, I could finally tune in to my gut and follow its guidance. Mind you, my gut didn't lay out a five year plan or anything like that.

Intuitively, I understood that if I followed the one thing I knew to be true - my love for Sean - that life would work itself out.

In less than a year from my resignation, I was moving out to San Francisco, California, to start my life on the West Coast with Sean, after a year and a half of making our long-distance relationship work.

All right, Gut, we're here in San Francisco... what's next?

Work - whether it was my academic studies or medical career - had always been synonymous with grinding, struggle, and delayed gratification. Finally, I had a chance to redefine what work meant to me, and my gut was telling me that I could actually find a way to do something fun! *Something fun? For work? *GASP**

Fitness was my anchor throughout my whole life - the one thing that grounded me, no matter how bad my circumstances were. The gym was my sanctuary, a sacred space where I could be completely present with myself - even when the wreckage of my life left me so distant from my core in every other way. Anytime I set foot in a gym, random people would always come up to me asking for advice... so, personal training was a perfect fit!

You might be thinking, "You went from being a doctor to a personal trainer?!" just as so many people questioned my judgment. But it made perfect sense to me, and that's all that mattered. The walls of perfectionism kept crumbling down, with each new decision that was guided by my gut.

It was almost too good to be true at first. I practically spent all my free time in the gym anyways... and now I could actually get paid to do it?! The pay wasn't great, but I'd take that any day over being in that miserable hospital again!

Within a year, it became quite obvious that I had so much more to offer than what the confines of the corporate gym environment allowed me to do. I wanted to go beyond the gym with my clients, to strengthen more than just their bodies. Fitness will only take you so far when your hormones are out of whack, your body is overwhelmed with toxins, or you're chronically inflamed from a poor diet and lifestyle. I knew I possessed the knowledge, tools, and passion to help people thrive in a way I didn't see modeled anywhere else around me.

I had learned not to delay when I realized something was holding me back from manifesting my true purpose.

So, it was time to move on. With no roadmap or blueprint in sight, my gut led me down the next imperfectly perfect leg of my journey...

I combined my passions of Medicine, fitness, and lifestyle coaching, and RIVA Wellness was born!

Radiant, Inspired, Victorious, Abundant Wellness.

Notice there is no 'P' for perfect anywhere in sight!

Yet, pieces were coming together perfectly! *Yes, I said "perfectly"!*

As fate would have it, I discovered a novel approach to Western Medicine called Functional Medicine, and I fell in love! Functional Medicine focuses on the whole person - mind, body, and spirit - and addresses the root causes of dysfunction, so people prevent and recover from chronic disease... and ultimately thrive. This is what I had been looking for all along!

Regardless of how many bumps in the road I have encountered (and there will surely be more to come), I can say wholeheartedly that I am grateful for every rocky step of my journey, and the way all of these moments have weaved together.

I am a less-than-perfect doctor, serving less-than-perfect people in a way that suits me perfectly.

All of my struggles and pain have played a perfect role in molding my heart so that I can empathize with people in the profound way that I do today. No experience has been in vain. I am perfectly imperfect... and imperfectly perfect. That's what makes me me, and I know that's more than enough!

More Than Enough Message #2
On Defeating the Not-Enoughness of Perfectionism

Wowee! This chapter was a doozie, wasn't it?

First, you should know that writing this chapter on perfectionism was one of the hardest things I've done in a really, really, really long time. It dragged on and on and on, making it quite clear that perfectionism has literally been the story of my life. Although it doesn't consume me as it has before, this manifestation of Not-Enoughness never goes away.

The writing process brought perfectionism bubbling back up to the surface in a very painful way. Reliving every challenging moment of my life and reflecting how each one was a blind pursuit of an unrealistic ideal - that is painful. Seeing how time and time again, I chased new ideals of perfection to compensate for my lack of self worth - that is painful. Feeling stuck while writing a chapter on perfectionism because you're obsessing over it being perfect, so it can resonate with your audience, so they can break free of perfectionism - that is painful... and painfully ironic.

Yet, there is hope in it all.

You are perfect in your imperfections. If you are a believer in Christ as I am, then hold fast to the idea that we are only made perfect through Him. He died in one of the most humiliating, excruciatingly painful manners possible, so we wouldn't have to spend our whole lives humiliating ourselves and living the excruciatingly painful existence of constantly chasing perfection.

It's time to let it all go. It's time to give yourself grace, and let yourself off the hook.

From a more universal perspective, striving for perfection can only carry you so far before it starts to break you down mentally, physically, and spiritually.

When this happens, the very thing you're working so friggin' hard for gets more and more out of reach. Talk about irony, right? And the more consumed you get with trying to be perfect, the more you forget how amazing you already are!

As you have seen in my story, perfectionism consumes us when we're focused on outside sources. When we are focused within, we know that we are perfectly worthy.

Don't believe me, perfectionist? Tell me, right now, 10 things you absolutely LOVE about yourself. I do this exercise with some of my clients, and you would think I was trying to yank their teeth out with a pair of pliers and no anesthesia!

I will give it a go first for you...

I love that I am a great writer, I'm compassionate, funny, kind-hearted. I'm a great cook. I'm in great shape. I'm easy going. I'm fun to be around. I have straight teeth. I love eating healthy. I'm a good listener...

There! I even timed myself, and it took 45.7 seconds to get all of that out on the page. And it was totally off the top of my head... if the random "straight teeth" comment didn't give that away!

So, how long will it take you to admit that you are already perfect in every way... just for being you?

Chapter 3: Settling For Less

I was born in 1986, which means I was a child of the 1990s Disney Renaissance, where every little girl dreamed that she was Ariel, Belle, or Jasmine. By the time I was four years old, I had the entire fantasy of meeting Prince Charming masterfully scripted and thoroughly rehearsed in my mind...

After a wicked tempest tore Prince Eric's ship to shreds, I pulled his lifeless body from the wreckage and swam him safely to shore.

Then, he regains consciousness as I sing the dulcet tones of an ancient mermaid healing song. The moment Prince Eric's eyes meet mine, we're instantly in love. Running his hand through my voluminous coral red hair, he pulls my face to his for a long, passionate kiss. A radiant white orb of light envelops us as the magic of our union transforms my mermaid tail into long, skinny, flawless legs. Suddenly, I'm robed in a pearly white ball gown and we're off to the castle to wed and have a peaceful dominion over all of the land and sea. And obviously, we lived happily ever after! *No need for that Ursula BS... this is my fantasy, after all!*

Ladies, don't leave me hanging here. I know I'm not the only one who had obscenely high standards for her romantic life before she ever got into a training bra.

Fast forward a decade, and at my high school, it seemed like I was the only girl doomed to walk the halls Prince Charming-less. *Just me again?* Growing up in a predominantly Caucasian town, I'd always been attracted to White boys - that's just what I knew. *I didn't see myself as being any different than them, but maybe that's just a filter you develop when you're always the token Black person wherever you go.*

However, it became impossible to notice that all the hunky boys I adored were dating the popular, skinny White girls, and I didn't fit any of those descriptors. So it was quite natural for me to conclude that I would never make the cut.

Then, there was Adam. He was one of the coolest, most lovable guys in high school... and he was the White, hunky, popular prototype than made him a real life Prince Eric. Somehow, he ended up becoming one of my best friends! We had the same twisted sense of humor and made fun of each other mercilessly, but in that classic, hilarious way high schoolers share affection with their closest friends. Any time we were together, I couldn't help but feel a sheer magnetism between us; there was no way he didn't feel it, too!

Of course he'll fall in love with me... maybe my actual romantic fantasy was more like a 1980s era John Hughes movie, where the handsome jock falls for the quirky, but kind-hearted girl that was under his nose the whole time! Ha! If only...

Soon after we graduated, I poured my entire bleeding heart out in a letter to Adam, confessing every ounce of my love to him. I bared my soul in such an intensely raw way, that I'm cringing now just thinking about it. I can't remember a single word I wrote, but I can still feel the tear-soaked keyboard under my trembling fingertips and my love-sick heart pounding in my chest... *this is my last chance!*

We were saying our final goodbyes the night before Adam left for college, and I nervously handed him the letter. "Please don't read it until later," I said.

Days go by. Weeks. Maybe months? Who knows. I honestly can't remember because it felt like my fate had been suspended in eternity.

I wish I had that old AOL Instant Messenger transcript to see what his exact response was, but it was something to the effect of, "Thanks, I really appreciated it." Or maybe it was something more to the tune of, "I really care about you, too"... again, my memory is cloudy (that's probably no coincidence). But it was nowhere near the Hollywood movie-scaled outpouring of love I had dreamed of!

Crash and burn went my heart. If someone like Adam who obviously felt something for me could so easily discard my heart, then there must not be any hope for me. *Maybe it's because I'm Black? If only I were skinnier... Maybe no one will ever want to be with me...*

Alas! The hopeless romantic in me wouldn't go down without a fight... she just lowered her standards to stay in the game.

What a perfect time to enter college.

Maybe the way to a college man's heart is just to get really plastered and throw yourself at him? ... Weird, that's not working... I thought guys loved easy, drunk girls, and yet they STILL don't want me?! There's something seriously wrong with me.

Perhaps fate might be turning in my favor? Shortly after graduating from college, Jacques came into the picture, and I thought my *Little Mermaid* fantasy was actually coming true! We met on the beach, and Jacques was as tall and handsome and as European as they come. *Imagine a blonde Prince Eric, but in a Speedo - yep, now that image is burned into your mind.* Jacques was charming, witty, and worldly, and actually attracted to me!

This is really my chance. I can't let this one go! And unfortunately, I lowered my standards once more to ensure the deal was sealed. I gave up the one thing I promised myself I'd save for my husband. Having grown up in the Church where celibacy was the ultimate virtue, shame, guilt, and disappointment flooded my heart.

But I kept all of those emotions dammed up by justifying that I was committed to marrying Jacques someday.

It wasn't long before his less attractive qualities surfaced, and even more shame, guilt, and disappointment swept in. The self-deprecating thoughts wouldn't leave my mind.

I never imagined I would ever be with someone who could be so hateful towards people, and yet, here I am.

I didn't like the person I had become... I didn't even recognize who I'd become. My identity had become so wrapped up in our dysfunctional relationship for almost three years. And what frustrated me the most was that I couldn't even blame him for it - I was the one who stuck around even though I didn't feel valued.

The sad reality was that I had stopped valuing myself.

I wish I could say that one morning I woke up and told myself, "Riva, you are an amazing, beautiful, precious soul, and you deserve to be treated like such. Break up with Jacques, and get on with your life."

No, no. Unfortunately that wasn't the case. I cheated on him.

To spare you all the graphic details, this other guy made me feel seen, appreciated, and valued in a way I hadn't felt in years. I was so desperate to feel good about myself again, and I was willing to cheapen myself for it. Yet again, settling for less than I deserve.

The funny thing is, that when you settle for less than you deserve from other people for so long, you follow suit with yourself, too.

It's a vicious cycle that keeps you running around in circles until you truly realize your worth, and stop spinning.

Needless to say, there was another heaping pile of shame, guilt, and disappointment that wiped me out.

And it also goes without saying, that Jacques and I had a rather ugly breakup. Worst of all, the things he said to me, I said 10 times worse to myself.

Why bother even trying to find Prince Charming anymore? All that brought me time and time again was shame, guilt, disappointment. I'm done with that!

At the time, I thought that just enjoying the moment with Prince Right Now would make me happy. I convinced myself that the fleeting pleasure of shallow encounters was all I needed, and that I was actually strong for not getting emotionally attached.

As you know, ladies, that doesn't work.

And every time a relationship didn't work out in my favor, I settled for less and less. Chip, chip, chipping away at my dignity and hardening my heart. *I wish I could slap some sense into my old self right now!*

In the midst of my self-sabotage, Sean came into my life, and everything was flipped upside down.

Up to this point, I had convinced myself that the greatest value I had to offer any man was my body, and I couldn't expect them to want anything more from me.

But with Sean, things seemed different. He asked me thoughtful questions. He seemed to care.

He actually wants to get to know me? He's drop dead gorgeous... and funny... and so incredibly kind to me. Oh, and he's talking about his mom a lot, that must mean he has good family values. This is too good to be true.

When he looked at me, I was totally disarmed, and his gaze penetrated the depths of my soul. *Ohhhhhh, THIS is what it feels like to be seen!*

When Sean looked at me, I didn't feel less than. I felt MORE than.

As much as I wanted to emotionally detach and protect myself, I felt a gentle nudging in my spirit to allow my poor hardened heart to soften. I was safe.

What happened next is impossible to describe.

Opening myself up to love again triggered something deep within me. I felt as if my soul was being rebooted or rewired. Something had shifted and awakened within me, and as uncomfortable as it was, I wanted to lean into it. After years of degrading myself, it was time to rebuild. I was ready.

I was ready, this time in the context of love, to defeat the Not-Enoughness.

But I didn't want to fix myself for Sean. I was fixing myself for me.

I needed to love myself first and foremost before I was worthy of any relationship. I wanted to feel worthy of all the love and happiness I longed for. And it all had to start with me.

Now, as I write this book five years later, I know that my life with Sean has been nothing short of a fairy tale.

Is it perfect? Hell to the no! But our love for each other grows more each day as we focus on our own ongoing healing. Our love is a force of nature - anyone who spends time with us can feel it.

Believe me: this is what's possible when you stop settling for less than you're worth.

<u>More Than Enough Message #3</u>
On Defeating the Not-Enoughness of Settling For Less

Okay, my friend, let's chat. I know this chapter has been all about how I was settling for less in my relationships, and maybe that really resonates with you.

But, this is about so much more than relationships; it's about your whole life. In what other ways are you settling for less than your worth? Maybe in your work? Or perhaps your health? I'm just throwing out a couple biggies I see in my clients' lives. Maybe it's something different for you.

Think about that scenario where you're settling for less. How does it make you feel about yourself? And how would you like to feel about yourself? Are they aligned? Probably not, right?

It's so ironic - we settle for less because we think we'll feel satisfied having *something* over nothing. But it comes at the price of compromising our values, which is a major insult to our sense of self worth.

Often, we end up settling again in vain efforts to compensate for that void, but our self worth ends up further in the hole. I know you're with me in this battle.

Friend: know your worth.

Know that you are enough.

Know that you are loved.

In fact, I want you to say it with me right now: "I am worthy. I am enough. I am loved."

When you use "I am" statements, you are speaking directly to your subconscious mind... your spirit...your soul. That is what needs to be rebooted and rewired in order to break out of the vicious cycle of settling for less.

Believe me, it's the hardest work you'll ever do to learn how to love yourself wholly and unconditionally. The work is never done. Just when you're sitting on top of the world admiring how friggin' amazing you are, something or someone comes out of nowhere to knock your legs out from under you. And you'll have to love yourself back to the top again. But if you know you're worthy, you'll quickly rise back where you belong.

You are worthy. You are enough. You are loved, my friend. Always remember that. Always, always, always remember that.

Chapter 4: Seeking External Validation

For most of my life, I trusted my parents' word as gospel, and surely, it was wise for me to do so in most cases. As you already learned earlier in this book, I wanted to be just like my Mom and Dad and would do anything to please them.

I love and respect my parents so incredibly much. I'd trust my life in their hands... *even if they weren't doctors!*

I'm all for honoring thy father and thy mother - I was raised in the Church, you know!

But, looking back now, I can see so many problems that arose when I dishonored myself, my desires, and my own ideas in exchange for their validation.

Take my college years for example. As a Kinesiology major, I absolutely fell in love with the human body from the exercise science perspective. I gained the tools to fuel, move, and sculpt my body into a healthy, strong physique and broke free from the prison of body hatred. I knew other captives out there who needed my help - *THAT was my calling... not Medicine!*

If only I could have intelligently articulated that to my parents.

I don't remember exactly what I said, when I told them I wanted to leave Medicine, but I do remember being a fumbling mess.

I can't... I just don't want to go to med school... but I actually really love what I'm doing right now... I know it's crazy... I... I... I don't know...

However, my memory is crystal clear when it comes to recalling my parents' response.

"And what do you actually think you're going to do?" they said. "You're not giving up your seat in med school... people would kill to be in your position!"

In the face of being challenged, I crumbled. I lost my backbone.

The idea of following a path my parents didn't support didn't even register on my mind as a possibility. I didn't even bother researching just how I might make a career out of exercise science so I could plead my case.

No, I accepted their word as gospel, assumed they knew what was best for me, and tried to forget I had any say in my own life. Heaven forbid, I let anything like my own passions threaten my position as the golden child!

No matter how much I tried, I couldn't ignore the gnawing sensation in my gut that there was something else out there for me. But what did my gut know? It didn't have the years of wisdom like my parents.

This knowingness in my gut became stronger and stronger all through medical school and my intern year. By the time I started my Preventive Medicine residency, my gut was flaring up at me. It knew what I needed to do, and I was ignoring it.

When am I going to start living my life for me? Enough is enough!

Fortunately, when I met Sean, the spiritual rewiring and rebooting that I went through applied to more than just my romantic life.

I was finally awake to the fact that I had more to live for than pleasing my parents... that I was worthy of my own desires... and that I alone was responsible for creating my best life.

"You're throwing your life away!" Mom proclaimed when I shared the news of my resignation.

Precisely, Mom. I'm throwing away my life *as I know it* to create a new one.

I won't lie - those words from my mother haunted me for a long, long time. But parents are only human and carry their own baggage, which can be projected on to their children. My Mom and I had something in common, though. She was the youngest child of her family as well, so she had faced a similar struggle of seeking validation from her own stern parents. I can now recognize her words, piercing as they were, came only from the lens of her own fears and insecurities, and out of wanting to keep me safe.

While my decision appeared reckless to her, my soul was at peace knowing I had made a calculated choice to live a life I could be proud of. It was me who had to face myself in the mirror each day, not my mom or anyone else.

If I make this sound like it's been easy, don't be mistaken.

In my years of charting my own path in Medicine, I had often shied away from discussing the details of my work with my parents. I simply didn't want to tread back into the waters of having to live up to the expectations I thought they had for me.

Just like every other manifestation of Not-Enoughness in this book, the struggle of seeking external validation never ceases. You simply get better at identifying it, calling it out for the joy-stealing imposter that it is, and taking the actions aligned with your own core values to defeat it.

More Than Enough Message #4
On Defeating the Not-Enoughness of Seeking External Validation

So, what have we learned here?

Life is wayyyyy better when you're living to meet your own approval first!

Yes, there is a natural inclination to please others that will never go away. I think there's a distinct biological reason for that, too. Behaving in compliance with societal norms has enabled us to thrive in communities since the dawn of man.

I'm not telling you to be totally self indulgent or to disregard how your actions impact others. That would be foolish. However, I am asking you to be a little more "selfish" and to think about what matters most to you.

Take a minute to deeply reflect on these questions: What is it that makes YOU happy? Are you actually doing what makes you happy? Is other people's happiness more important than your own? Is prioritizing others' happiness over your own improving your own life? Then why do you keep seeking their approval?

You see what I'm getting at, don't you? It all comes back to self-worth.

You must know that you are worthy of a happy, fulfilled life.

You don't have to live as a martyr, constantly sacrificing yourself so others can be more satisfied with themselves. You deserve better than that!

If the person you seek to please truly loves you, they will still love you even if you choose a path divergent to what they see for you. Sometimes it may strain the relationship, but if this person is worth having in your life, the two of you will work through it.

No matter what you do, people are always going to have an opinion about you and your choices. Their opinions of you do not define you. When you become fully rooted in your intrinsic value, the most important opinion is that of the person looking back at you in the mirror.

Your own validation is more than enough, beautiful soul, and don't you ever forget that.

Chapter 5: Denying Your Dreams

As a little girl, I loved doing chores around the house so I could earn some spending money. You see, my parents did not believe in giving us an allowance just for the sake of it. One time I asked if I could get $10 for every 'A' on my report card like my friend Chelsea, and Mom straight up laughed in my face.

"Why should I be paying you for something you should already be doing?" said Mom. "Money is to be earned!"

I didn't let that stop me! I could figure out how to provide value in exchange for the things I wanted!

Oh, the new Gymnast Barbie is out! Mom, can I pull the weeds in the yard for $20?

Oversized gardening gloves and hand shovel in tow, I worked tirelessly until every wayward sprig was plucked from the ground. Sweat streaming down my face, with hands aching and chafed, I was fueled by my fantasy of twirling Gymnast Barbie "Jimmie" (*as I would name her, of course*) through the air in the most astounding tumbling passes anyone had ever seen.

Come later that day, I was beaming with the pride of a thousand peacocks as I poured my piggy bank out over the toy store counter, stacked my stray coins, unfolded each crumpled dollar, and claimed my dream toy. The hard work paid off!

We can learn so much from our childhood selves, right?

Put many of us, as adults, in that same Gymnast Barbie scenario, and here is how it would go...

Dude, I really want that Gymnast Barbie, she's so cool! But, my yard is soooo big, and there's a ton of weeds! That's going to take forever! And what if there are snakes or wasps or other creatures out in those flower beds? Oh, I just got a manicure, and this is going to ruin my nails! And what if I get the Barbie, and she breaks? Who am I to want Gymnast Barbie when I have other Barbies? I should just be happy with what I have. Ah, forget about it.

We find excuses. We discount our desires. We deny our dreams, no matter how big or how small. We say they're not worth it when, in truth, we're saying *we* are not worth it. *Now let that sink in.*

But, don't worry, I have one final story of my own personal failure in this "dream denying" department to make you feel better.

The enterprising spirit that I have always been, I seized a rather unlikely business opportunity in my year off between college and medical school.

I started a Mary Kay business! And, I say "unlikely," because I never even wore makeup, I didn't like the color pink, and I'd never even tried the products. But something in my spirit told me to go for it, I dove in head-first, and something sprang awake inside of me!

I felt the most confident, creative, purpose-driven, and fulfilled I had ever been in my entire life. I quickly rose to the top as one of the leading team builders in my unit, and I found success around every corner.

This newly discovered freedom of being my own boss was beyond exhilarating - who knew work could be so fun?! Nothing compared to the joy of empowering women to create financial independence and witnessing their self worth skyrocket in the process. I didn't feel scammy or spammy - *we all know that stereotype of direct marketers* - because I saw genuine transformation blossoming in the lives around me that

I impacted through my business. I never wanted it to end.

It was a race against the clock to earn my pink Mary Kay Cadillac within the year before medical school would start to take over my life.

But, if I can make a career out of this, maybe I won't have to go to med school after all! I would still be changing people's lives, but I would have the quality of life I'd always wanted... AND the added bonus of doing something I loved!

As time started to run out, self doubt and fear insidiously crept in, and my confidence sheepishly slipped away. *What if Mary Kay doesn't work out? What will people think of me if I turn my back on Medicine for Mary Kay? My parents would literally kill me! But, what if I could do both? No, that's crazy, I'd never have the time...*

So, with all of these thoughts swirling in my brain, I did what any "rational" person would do. I gave up my hot pink pipe dreams, started medical school, and endured the next four years, as you know, kicking and screaming every step of the way.

For years, I never understood why this defeat wounded me so deeply.

Mary Kay had never been a part of my plan. It didn't make sense for someone with a promising future in Medicine to throw it all away. I wasn't even making that much money yet, anyway.

Only recently did it dawn on me: that in the process of diving into being my own boss with Mark Kay, I had gotten a small taste of my dream - to build a business I love. To serve, empower, and help women heal, all while creating an expansive, joy-filled life.

Then, in an instant, I had thrown it all away like it never mattered.

And here's what I believed: I didn't think I *deserved* to have it all.

I wasn't willing to sacrifice the prestigious title of "doctor" because I felt my value came from my social status. I didn't think the contribution I was already making into other people's lives was "good enough" because I still didn't think I was "good enough."

You've already seen how this story ends. Thankfully, everything still worked out in my favor. *Hooray, I still get to have it all!*

Looking back now, I don't regret one bit that I chose Medicine, because I know I'm called to be a healer.

What I do regret is that I couldn't love myself enough to fight for my dream, that my own happiness didn't matter enough for me to protect it, and that I didn't stand up for what I loved when it stood in the crossfire.

I can tell you one thing, though: I will never deny my dreams ever again because I know that my life, my family's life, and everyone I may possibly impact in my lifetime, is worth it!

More Than Enough Message #5
On Defeating the Not-Enoughness of Denying Your Dreams

Alright, peeps. Let's break this one down a little further...

How many of you as kids said, "When I grow up, I want to work really, really hard in a job I don't love, and hopefully I get paid poorly and have a horrible quality of life, too!" ?

Nope. None of us. Our imaginations ran free, and we didn't think for a second whether our dreams were rational or not! We imagined living in an epic mansion with a petting zoo and rollercoasters in the backyard. We'd play all day, never have a bedtime, and it would be summer vacation all year round.

Then came that catastrophic day when we stopped dreaming...

Do you remember that day? Maybe someone put you in a box and told you that those were the limits of you capabilities? Or maybe it was your own fear that paralyzed you and destroyed your hope of a brighter future? Maybe you had already tried and failed... and tried and failed again... so you accepted defeat and sent your dreams to their final resting place.

Now, obviously my childhood dream scenario isn't the most feasible, but I bet you have other very conceivable fantasies that you could actually bring to life.

Your dreams were divinely planted in your mind, because only YOU have the unique gifts to make them happen.

When you deny your dreams, it's like denying life to a part of your soul. Not only does it suffocate your self expression, but it also sends your self worth spiraling further into the ground.

So, don't be disheartened when your dreams don't make sense to other people.

Your dreams will only make sense to them when you actualize that dream, and they see it with their own two eyes. Take this book for example. The people who once questioned my bizarre career choices can now see clearly that this was part of my purpose all along.

It's up to you to capture the essence of that dream in your mind so vividly that you can taste it, see it, smell it, feel it, and hear it like it's right in front of your face. You must love and nurture that dream like it's your baby and protect it from all who may do it harm.

Imagine your dream is your favorite movie that's playing on repeat on the screen of your mind. Every time your mind wanders or you drift off to sleep, you enter this new world of your wildest wishes fulfilled. Your heart swells with overwhelming emotion because you know it's only a matter of time before this reality materializes.

Only when you become invested in that process is it absolutely impossible to deny your dreams.

There is one critical component to all of this: your self image. If you're waiting for your dreams to come true to feel worthy, you've got it all backwards.

I admit, this has been the hardest thing for me to conquer, and my work is not yet done. It is ongoing.

You must believe you already are that extraordinary person who has achieved your dreams... because you are! Your genetic makeup doesn't suddenly morph to give you superpowers to accomplish your goals. No! Those innate gifts are already within you.

So tell me, how much would you love and honor and respect yourself if you knew you'd already achieved massive success? A whole friggin' lot, right? You would go the extra mile for yourself. You would stand up for yourself. You would show yourself immense compassion and grace. You would forgive yourself. You would listen to yourself. And you would never deny yourself the joy of fulfilling your wildest dreams.

So dream big, my worthy friends, your destiny awaits!

Section 2:

There is More Beyond Not-Enoughness

Chapter 6: What is More?

I recognize that it may be a stretch to truly believe with every part of your being that you are more than enough. It took me almost 30 years to reach that conclusion, so it would be naive of me to expect you to hop on board in the few short hours of reading this book. Perhaps it's easier for you to identify that you are seeking More in some shape or form.

Let's explore that...

More is a very tricky concept. Unfortunately, many of us have fallen into the trap of thinking that More means having to *do more* or *acquire more* to compensate for our inadequacies. This is a direct result of Not-Enoughness. Don't buy into that fallacy.

In its simplest form, More is all about growth. As spiritual beings, our souls are constantly seeking greater expansion and fulfillment. But when we're trapped by Not-enoughness in any of its manifestations, we stagnate at best, and more often than not, we deteriorate. Obviously, deterioration is the polar opposite of growth.

The five chapters you just read, detailing the major breakdowns in my life, serve as evidence of this.

Let me clarify this concept with an example: I'm sure you've had an experience with work where you weren't being challenged enough, right? And how did you feel? Bored. Frustrated. Stifled. Or to put it in a simple utterance: *meh*. Not a single one of us was created to have a "meh" kind of life. No! We were designed to seek knowledge, create opportunities, and face obstacles in order to expand the very nature of our being. In short, we were created for "More."

More is also about achieving greater self-awareness. *Do you really understand yourself?*

I surely didn't understand myself for most of my life. How can we love someone or something we don't understand? It's impossible! I hated my body until I gained an understanding of how it worked. You'll never conquer Not-Enoughness and enter the realm of More until you understand who you are. Don't be afraid to do the deep self-exploratory work like I was at that time. Yes, you will uncover some ugly truths about yourself in the process, but you will also gain an awareness of how to overcome them.

More is that nudging in your spirit... the gnawing in your belly... that small, quiet voice in your head telling you to take that leap into the unknown. You might know it as listening to your gut or trusting your intuition. But just as self awareness begets self love, it also begets a heightened intuition. You know how you can pick out a loved one's voice in a crowd because you're so attuned to them? The same applies with your gut, too. Be patient, though - it takes time and practice to sharpen this sense to laser precision. When you can accurately decipher the signals your gut sends you, you're on an unobstructed path to living your truth.

Ah yes, "living your truth," or simply put, **being you**.

Without the heavy burdens of Not-enoughness, the real you emerges. You shine like never before. You are a beacon of light, attracting all of your deepest desires into your life.

Flow is your natural state.

It's not that life suddenly becomes easy - no, that's not the case - but you begin to face each challenge with ease, having complete confidence in your ability to conquer anything.

You stand humbly, yet fiercely in your power. You let your voice be heard without having to speak over others.

You are comfortable walking in your own shoes and never think twice about how fast or slow people walk around you.

You are simply you... and happy to be you... growing more into the fullest version of you each day. You realize you were the More you were always seeking.

Which brings us full circle back to the fact that you always have been, already are, and forever will be more than enough.

Chapter 7: Implementing M.O.R.E.

When I reflect upon this wild journey that has been my life, I can see clearly now how I have hungered for More every step of the way. More is the antithesis of Not-Enoughness. But if you don't know you deserve More, then you unwittingly fall prey to the trap of Not-Enoughness, as I did time after time.

This led me to start thinking creatively about how I could introduce More to more people. As a result, I came up with the **M.O.R.E. Framework**.

M.O.R.E. stands for these four action steps:

> **M** - Create a **Mindset** of Success
> **O** - Take **Ownership** of Your Circumstances
> **R** - **Restore** the Foundations of Your Health
> **E** - Enhance Your **Energy**

MINDSET

Create a Mindset of Success

I know I'm not telling you anything new when I say that mindset is everything. We know this, yet we struggle to positively direct our thinking so that it actually works in our favor. Thus, I'm going to put you to work by teaching you four success mindset strategies that have continuously benefited both me and my clients. *Time to get out your pen and paper!*

1. Understand the problem from 360 degrees and know that there is always a solution. One question I love to ask myself when I feel stuck is, "What would the person who's already solved this problem do?" I know this seems over-simplified, but I promise it works. Sometimes we're just too close to the problem to see the solution. Stepping back into someone else's shoes widens our lens and can bring the solution into full focus.

2. Approach yourself with curiosity over condemnation. It's easy to get into the bad habit of looking at your problems and beating yourself up for them. Let's stop that! Instead, have a curious mind as to why it is you find yourself in a particular situation. Reflect quietly, tune into your emotions and your intuition, and see what comes up for you. You'll be astounded by the insights that will bubble to the surface of your mind when you show yourself a little compassion.

3. Have a crystal clear vision of what you want.
Get specific about what you want in your life, but don't get caught up in obsessing over how you'll make it happen. That will come with time, I promise you. Write about your vision with all of the vivid sensory details of the experiences that you want to create. Visualize it constantly. Create affirmations around it. Imagine that you are already the person who has achieved all of your dreams, *because you are* - the circumstances just haven't materialized yet. Ask yourself: What actions would that person take on a daily basis? What kind of people would they surround themselves with? How would they speak, dress, walk, and interact with the world around them?

4. Embrace failure. The most successful people are also the ones who have failed the most, and in some of the most costly ways. Remember that the sooner you fail and figure out what doesn't work, the sooner you can figure out what does work. If you delay taking action because you're afraid of failing, then you're only delaying success. Shift your thinking, and start seeing failure as a success-enabling tool. On the flip side of this, celebrate each and every one of your wins. Even the small ones... especially the small ones! At the end of the day, make a list of all of your wins. Hey, it could be as simple as: "I got out of my pajamas today." *That's a big one for me because I work from home!* In celebrating your wins, the failures don't seem as significant. I guarantee, if you're properly keeping track, you'll find you have way more wins than failures in any given day!

OWNERSHIP
Take Ownership of Your Circumstances

I have good and bad news for you... I'll get the bad out of the way first: **You are the only person responsible for your circumstances.** That's not to say you are to blame for anything, but it is up to you to redirect your life if you don't like the trajectory you're on.

Now, for the good news: **You are the only person responsible for your circumstances.** *Gotcha!* This isn't just good news - it's fantastic news! You are not a victim, and you don't have to rely on anybody else to change your life. You have all the power to steer your life exactly where you want to go.

But first, we have to get past one obstacle: *you.*

To help us with this, there are three patterns to address that may prevent you from positively shifting your life circumstances.

1. **You make excuses.** I'm too busy... I don't have the money... I don't know how. *Sound familiar?* All of these excuses can feel valid, but they're still excuses, so we're going to use that solution-oriented success mindset you have now adopted to move past them!

   "I'm too busy" = I'm prioritizing my time on other things. Make a list of everything that's demanding of your time. Then mark next to those items "keep," "delegate," or "downgrade." Be brutally honest in your evaluation. Between the delegated and downgraded items, you should be able to clear up enough space on your schedule to add in more important tasks.

   "I don't have the money" = I'm prioritizing my money on other things. I know finances are a touchy subject, but hear me out. Even if you're living paycheck to paycheck, I bet you have periodic small expenses that add up. That daily Starbucks run? That can add up to $100+ per month. Weekly manicure? Another $100 per month. Still subscribing to cable? I think I've made my point...

"I don't know how" = *I haven't prioritized learning how yet.* Everything you could possibly want to know is on Google. Need human help? Ask! There must be someone among your family, friends, or your extended network who has the expertise you are looking for and would love to support you.

2. **You become complacent.** Things aren't severe enough for you to want to take action, but you're not happy where you are either. I see this come up all the time with my clients' health. They are frustrated because they are not losing any weight, but when I suggest cutting out alcohol, sugar, and refined carbohydrates, the wall goes up.
    So, it's time to choose: will you be complacent or committed?

    It's challenging to break the inertia of inaction, but the only way to gain momentum is to start somewhere. If you're feeling overwhelmed, it's helpful to pick one simple habit to adopt. Staying with the weight loss example, maybe that one simple habit is giving up drinking alcohol during the week. It's not a huge sacrifice, but once you build confidence adhering to one habit, you can introduce other habits and continue to build on them.

3. **You don't plan.** I know you've heard the saying: "If you fail to plan, plan to fail." Let's continue with the weight loss example and say that your spouse or your friend is taking you out to an Italian dinner on a Friday night. If you show up without a plan, chances are you will fall back into your old habits, and eat most of the breadsticks before your meal even arrives, have a couple glasses of wine, and order your all-time fave - the fettuccine alfredo (of course with extra breadsticks to sop up all of that extra sauce!) Or, you can enter the evening having previously reviewed the menu for its healthiest options. Since it's the start of the weekend, you choose to indulge in wine, but restrain yourself to one glass. You avoid the breadsticks altogether because you know once you get started, it's all over, and you're perfectly satisfied with your fish served over a bed of sauteed veggies... and the few bites of pasta you stole off of your date's plate. *What a difference having a plan can make, right?*

So tell me, which one of those three patterns sounds most like you? And what are the first steps you need to take to break those patterns?

RESTORE

As a physician and coach who specializes in holistic wellness, I focus on four key areas as the foundation of health: **diet, exercise, sleep, and stress management.** If we all knew how to properly balance these lifestyle factors, or the **"Core Four"** as I call them, we would practically eradicate chronic disease. In fact, there are certain groups of people who have done just that, like the inhabitants of the "Blue Zones" of the world, where the world's healthiest people have been found to live. Due to their healthy lifestyles in these areas, they have the lowest rates of chronic disease and the highest number of people who are one hundred or more years old.

First up, diet.

Is your diet providing a healthy balance of nutrients to sustain and fortify you? Not sure? How do you feel soon after you eat? Do you feel sluggish or do you feel revitalized? That gives you a good indication of how your diet is serving you.

Think about it this way: the foods you eat are broken down into the building blocks by which your body repairs itself. Would you rather rebuild your body out of junk yard rubbish or construction grade materials?

Yes, you could end up spending more money on higher quality foods, but if you haven't embraced it by now, I'll say it again: *You are worth it!*

To put it another way, you can pay now, or pay a whole lot more with interest later. What do I mean by this? If you're eating cheap, unhealthy foods now, over your lifetime, you'll be spending much more on medical bills to treat the chronic diseases you develop.

On to exercise...

Uh oh, you're getting squirmy over there! Not a fan? I'll rephrase it then: movement. You don't have to go to a gym every day, but you do need to make time for purposeful movement throughout your day. This could be as simple as walking 20 minutes - it doesn't have to be complicated.

The sheer fact that most of your body weight is comprised of muscle mass proves that you were designed to move.

Your body is an immaculate work of mobile art. The more it moves, the more of that natural beauty is reflected in your physique. And let's not forget the numerous health benefits of movement, ranging from increased longevity, improved brain health, decreased rates of cancer, and much more.

So if the thought of exercising, or moving more, makes you cringe, let's make it more appealing. What do you actually enjoy doing? Dancing? Playing with your kids? Maybe you can dust off the old roller skates? Use your imagination!

Try this to get started: Choose 2-3 fun ways you like to move. Set a 20-minute date with yourself, and yes, put it on your calendar each day. Then, get moving that magnificent body of yours!

Now, on to sleep...

Ahhh, glorious sleep! Are you getting enough? Note: the average range is 7 to 9 hours per night, but you probably have an idea of what that optimal range is for you. For me, it's 7.5 hours.

Unfortunately, when our schedules become more demanding, sleep is often the first thing to go out the window. I beg of you, please don't fall into the habit of sacrificing sleep long-term.

Not only is sleep deprivation one of the major risk factors for the development of Alzheimer's Disease, but it's also critical for your short term cognitive performance.

You know that zombie feeling you have when you've stayed up most of the night before? Ideas are slower to reach your mind, your memory is fuzzy... it's almost like half of your brain was replaced with cotton candy.

Brain health aside, sleep is critical for healing and growth, immune system activation, a healthy metabolism, mental and emotional health, and many of the functions that enable you to thrive.

Here are my key sleep tips for you: Try to establish a regular bedtime, ideally by 10 p.m. This isn't just for the kiddos! It's important for regulating your circadian rhythms and sleep cycle. Power down your devices at least an hour before bedtime, and keep them out of the bedroom - the UV light emitted from them will prevent melatonin secretion, making it harder for you to fall asleep. If you can, take naps! (Though I know some of you are physically unable to during the day.) *This book has literally been fueled by naps... I just woke up from a rather glorious one!* When you are sleep deprived, naps will help you pay off your sleep debt.

Last, but definitely not least, let's chat about stress management.

Unfortunately, we live in a world where we'll never get rid of stress. *Even if my dream came true to live on the beach in Bora Bora, stress would still hunt me down and find me there!*

You might not know this, but stress is what drives most disease processes. It triggers inflammation, which in turn damages your tissues and disrupts the proper functioning of every system in your body. De-stressing isn't a luxury; it is equally as vital for your survival as eating or sleeping. But because the effects of stress are gradual, they often go unseen until manifesting as something that sends you to the doctor.

Everything boils down to how we manage stress. Be proactive. Do you regularly integrate some kind of stress release practice into your life? *That massage you had six months ago doesn't count!*

You could combine exercise and stress management into a mindful movement practice like yoga, Tai Chi, or Qi Gong.

I'm also a huge believer in the power of meditation. Did you know it actually increases your brain volume and helps rewire your brain for a greater sense of purpose and joy in your life? How cool is that?!

Here's what I recommend: have something small you do for yourself on a daily basis - journaling, reading, yoga... you decide. It doesn't have to take more than 5-10 minutes. Actually, the shorter the better - it will be easier to commit to on a daily basis. Then, have something bigger you do for yourself on a weekly basis.

I have "Feel Good Fridays" where I implement some type of self-care therapy: I may sit in the hot tub, go to the spa, see the chiropractor or acupuncturist, or do float tank therapy... whatever makes me feel good! All week long, I'm motivated by the fact that come Friday, I have an afternoon all to myself to rejuvenate my mind and body. *Go ahead, you're welcome to steal this idea!*

So, which one of the "Core Four" is most out of balance for you? Diet? Exercise? Sleep? Stress Management?

Start with one of them and focus your energy there. Don't try to do a total lifestyle overhaul all at once! That's probably why you've given up so many times in the past, right? Allow yourself to take small steps and naturally progress.

By doing this, you will restore the foundations of your health, and fill your body with life. You will enable your body to heal itself. You will fine-tune the channels of communication between your mind and your body. All of this enables you to experience a sense of wholeness within your spirit, where you can't help but feel like you are more than enough!

ENERGY
Enhance Your Energy

Let's take a deep breath together. Breathe in. Breathe out. *Ahhhhh.* We're in the final stretch of M.O.R.E. and I want us to end our journey on a high note. This section is all about enhancing our energy, so let's keep the vibes high!

Energy is the life force that powers us, and the currency we exchange with the world around us. It includes everything in our internal and external environments that dictates how we feel physically, emotionally, and spiritually.

That deep breath you just took? That was a calming, yet invigorating surge of energy, right? *If you didn't notice anything, try again and really tune into what your body is experiencing.* My jaw unclenches, my tight shoulders drop, and a gently electrifying pulse sweeps across my skin. My body is reassured that it is safe as my breath flips the switch on my nervous system's rest and digest pathway, or "low power mode."

The air we breathe, the food we eat, the relationships we're in, the home we live in, the work we do, the experiences we partake in - they all influence how we feel. If you don't enjoy the emotional or physical energy states that these things impart on you, it's up to you to change them. *Job draining the life out of you? Why are you staying there?!*

Here's an experiment for you: go through the rest of today with your "energy sensors" turned on.

Remember, More is about increasing your self awareness. Take note of the situations where you're in a good mood and full of energy. What are you doing? Where are you? Who are you with? What time of day is it? What are you wearing? Take a 360 degree mental snapshot of the entire scenario. And, likewise, take note of the opposite - when your mood and energy levels tank. What were those circumstances? This provides you with valuable insight into how you operate optimally, so you are never again a victim of the energy vampires around you.

Unfortunately, many of us are in a constant energy crisis because we spend our precious energy on relationships, jobs, and experiences that don't replete us. They deplete us. And from the biological perspective, the battery of the human cell - the mitochondria - even loses its power and dies due to the toxic, draining effects of stress. And guess what: mitochondrial dysfunction is another one of the major underlying factors in chronic disease. That's the ultimate energy crisis threatening our society!

So, what's the solution? Seek more of what makes you feel whole!

Nourish your body with foods and your soul with friends who uplift you. Follow what makes your heart sing and your feet dance. Do more of what makes you feel alive, because physically, emotionally, and spiritually, it's doing just that.

My friend, you deserve to live your life feeling every ounce of the high-powered force of nature that you truly are, and have always been.

Why?

Say it with me: Because you are MORE THAN ENOUGH!

Chapter 8: My Final Words to You

My dear, dear friend, I may not know you or the exact situation you're in, but I know your pain. I'm quite convinced that the root of most human suffering is that we think we're not good enough. Please know that Not-enoughness is the biggest lie that ever existed!

It's not an easy journey to reclaim your worthiness, but you will get there. Along the way, I have had to lean on many coaches and mentors who believed in me when I couldn't believe in myself. Let me be that person for you now. I am here, asking you to lean on my utmost belief in you.

You've been destined for greatness before you were even a distant spark in the universe. You can and *will* overcome every obstacle in your life. Your struggles, your pain, your failures - they are your strength. I promise you.

Would you believe that I used to be ashamed to share my story? And here I am writing a whole book about it! Not only has this experience facilitated my own ongoing healing, but I know it will also help you and many others to heal. No struggle, pain, or failure is in vain, should you choose to use it for good.

So, my dear friend, what you do from here is up to you.

Are you ready to leave Not-Enoughness in the past where it belongs? Are you ready to step into More, experience remarkable growth, and soar through life at new heights?

You don't have to be perfect. You don't even have to know the way. You simply need to believe and embrace that you are **more than enough**. Then, your very own journey to love yourself, listen to your gut, and live your truth will unfold from there.

YOU'VE GOT THIS!

Sending you all my love,

Dr. Riva

Made in the USA
Lexington, KY
26 October 2019